I0365121

Mentoring Myths

Unlock 6 mentoring myths to reenergize your thinking, and launch you into overwhelming success

By Michael "Dr. Rod" Rodriguez, Ed.D.

Copyright ©2019 Michael P. Rodriguez

Published by Marmic Business Consulting, LLC
Port Reading, NJ 07064

All Rights Reserved.
In Accordance with U.S. Copyright of 1976, the scanning, uploading, and electronic sharing of any part of this book without permission of the publisher, constitutes unlawful piracy and theft of the author's intellectual property.

Mentoring Myths is a registered trademark of
Michael P. Rodriguez
ISBN: 978-1-7334542-0-9
978-1-7334542-1-6

Dedication

To every reader of this book,
may it liberate your mind, loose your spirit,
and unleash you to be your best self.

Table of Contents

Preface iii

Introduction v

Opening Thoughts viii

Mentee Myths 2

    Mentoring Myth 1: 4

    Mentoring Myth 2 12

    Mentoring Myth 3 20

    Mentoring Myth 4 26

Mentor Myths 32

    Mentoring Myth 5 33

    Mentoring Myth 6 40

Bonus Chapter 45

Acknowledgements 49

About the Author 51

A Few of My Mentees 53

Preface

I've been writing the physical copy of this book for about a year but the truth is the fruition of this book has taken over ten years to develop. It is the culmination of years of hands-on experience serving as a mentor to dozens of students for almost twenty years in education, as well as my experience directing a mentoring program with hundreds of students, staff, and administrators. My experience as a mentor has been poured into this book, and although the cases are fictionalized, the myths are real and stem from my professional experience.

It has been a cathartic experience. I often tell others; I consider the work I do as grassroots; on the ground; people work. It is a "trench" work. I help people through a variety of issues and concerns, and many times see them in extremely vulnerable moments. Throughout the various programs I've led, I have travailed with the students; I've laughed, cried, celebrated their victories, and consoled them in their pain. When speaking about mentoring publicly, I tell the audience that great mentors, give the sum of themselves. You may ask, what do I mean by that? A great mentor does not simply pass on knowledge. They freely share all their knowledge and experiences to help someone else learn from the totality of their life experiences. **Mentoring makes a difference and I believe everyone should be mentored.**

This book is by no means exhaustive. There are dozens of myths about how to choose a mentor, who qualifies as a mentor, as well as what mentors do, and I've only listed a handful. This book is designed to get the reader, thinking about how to cast away any doubt about finding and utilizing a mentor.

Believe me, there are dozens of men and women in your life right now who want to pour into you but you need to be open to receive what they have to offer. Having mis-understandings about mentorship can be a blockade to connecting with someone. I want to take away those blockers, barriers, hesitations or misgivings you have about mentorship.

Each chapter can be read individually or in succession. They are designed to give an overview, example, and conclusion regarding a specific myth I've encountered in my work in mentoring programs.

Again, this is not a complete list of mentoring myths but I believe if this book can guide one person into a healthy mentoring relationship, it has fulfilled its purpose. My desire is that this book helps breakdown a few myths about mentoring, and opens a new world of success for you.

Introduction

What is a mentor? Mentoring has been around for thousands of years in one form or the other and many people when they think about mentoring, there is no succinct answer to what it is, however, undoubtedly, there seems to have always been a need for mentorship. I believe that to understand what mentoring is we must begin at the beginning.

The term "mentor" has existed for almost three thousand years. The origin of the term stems from Homer's Odyssey. In the story, Odysseus, the king of Ithaca, while fighting in the Trojan War, entrusts the care of his household to Mentor. Mentor also serves as the teacher, guide, and overseer of Odysseus' son, Telemachus. After the war, Telemachus, now grown, ventures out in search for his father. Athena, the Goddess of War, assumes the form of Mentor and accompanies Telemachus on his quest, providing the wisdom of the gods as he searches for his father. The word Mentor evolved to mean a trusted adviser, friend, teacher, and wise person.

Mentorship has taken many forms over the past three thousand years but has always inferred to one person helping another person reach a goal and when done right, it works. Mentoring is a proven way to reach personal, group, and organizational goals. It is one of the unsung tools that everyone should have in their arsenal.

Mentoring has far-reaching implications. The impact made by mentors often echo in the lives of their mentees for years and when done extremely well, those who have been mentored often become mentors, passing on the knowledge they gained.

I have personally benefited from mentoring throughout my academic and professional career. Much of the advice offered to me positioned me to take a risk, reconsider the direction I was moving in, recalculate my plans, and ultimately propelled me into my future. When I think back to the critical times in my life, somewhere in the story was someone who mentored me. There were times when I was offered advice from a potential mentor and I didn't listen. When I consider why I didn't listen, I must admit, sometimes it was ego, some was bad timing, and other times I just didn't understand what was happening. The truth is I simply didn't know I was being mentored. Instead of understanding that someone was trying to mentor me, I questioned the advice. This is why I wrote this book. My misunderstanding about the mentoring process stopped me from accepting good advice and great opportunities, and I do not want that to happen to another person. I allowed my myths about mentoring to hold me back.

Friends, life is short and we should be willing to take advantage of every opportunity presented to us. My belief in many of the myths listed below held me back when I was in the midst of a mentoring moment. I want you to make the most out of every piece of advice you receive from a mentor, whether in a formalized mentoring relationship or you find yourself being mentored in a moment of random conversation.

Opening Thoughts

The Why

Who is this book written for? Who is the target audience? "Everyone!" my ego screams. Yes, I would be the first person in history to truly write a book for everyone on the planet. Only in my dreams.

When I considered writing this book, I struggled with these questions: Is this book for mentors? Is it for mentees? Is it for professionals well into their career, or for a high school student getting ready to be ushered into adulthood? Who could benefit from this book? After a while I realized I was overthinking it. I just needed to write the book.

As I began, I couldn't help but think about my own motivation. Why did I need to write this book? What was driving me to push this project out into the world? Then it hit me, this book was for me. There was a time that I desperately needed this information but didn't realize it. To know my story is to know that there was a time when I lived with no direction, no opportunities and no hope. I wrote this book for the 20-year-old me, who lived as if tomorrow didn't matter, and needed some direction but didn't know how to get it.

What would I want the 20-year-old me to know? Here it is. I've had the privilege of currently working with many 18 to 25-year-olds in my daily vocation.

Just as I needed this information some 25 years ago, I know so many in this generation can use and need this information now. This is the population the book is penned to reach and touch. The thousands of young men and women who need a push, prod, poke or a positioning to point them in the right direction.

Will this book help someone who is not a young adult? Absolutely! I meet so many not-so-young adults who have never benefited from the blessing of mentorship. Like myself, so many older adults missed opportunities because of the lack of understanding about mentoring. But the good news is, it's not too late. Use the tools in this book to its fullest. Dig through the pages and take action! Actionable steps are placed at the end of each chapter and I encourage you to go for it! Implement each step and start living the life you want by using the power of mentorship.

If you have questions, contact me at:

info@dr-rod.com.

Mentee Myths

men·tee
/menˈtē/

noun
noun: **mentee**; plural noun: **mentees**
1. a person who is advised, trained, or counseled by a mentor.

"Our chief want in life is somebody who will make us do what we can."

— Ralph Waldo Emerson

Mentoring Myth 1

Choose A Mentor Based on Their Bank Account

Choosing a mentor takes time. It should not be done quickly or without thought. A serious mentee should develop a checklist of what they are looking for in a mentor. The financial statement of the mentor shouldn't be top of the list. If the criteria for selecting a mentor only includes how much money the mentor makes or their net worth, you can miss out on the larger benefits of mentoring. Mentors can give you the advice to help you make money, but what a mentor gives you is way more important than money.

"Get Dat Money …"

I asked a diverse room of roughly 30 young people this question, "Who would you love to mentor you?" Hands shot up quickly, I pointed around the room collecting names; names like Jay-Z, Sean "Diddy" Combs, Bill Gates, Beyoncé, and Warren Buffet all rang out.

I smiled leaned on the podium and began, "These men, like many moguls of our time, have become synonymous with success. Books have and will be, written about them. Their daily moves are chronicled in the pages of media. They are the first "titans of industry" of the 21st century. But how do we know they will make good mentors?"

I scanned the room after posing my question. A few hands shot up quickly. They were ready to answer. I glanced over the faces and could see their young minds turning my question over and over reluctant to offer an opinion lest this is an intellectual trap.

I pointed at Sam who was patiently and eagerly waiting.

"Okay, Sam, let's hear your answer," I stated.

Sam answered, "Rich people always make great mentors, and they can teach you how to get that money." He shimmied in his chair side to side, showing pleasure with his answer.

"Interesting answer, Sam, and a common one, as many people do believe that men and women who have garnered a certain amount of wealth are great mentors, but let's look at this deeper."

A mentor should have a measurable degree of success. No one wants to glean from someone who has not achieved more than they have and I believe the minimum standard for choosing a mentor should be finding someone who is doing or has done something you want to achieve. Successful mentors don't always need to have made tons of money. Does it help in adding credibility? Absolutely! The fact that someone has done well financially, bolsters their claims that they have a knowledge base and ratifies the effectiveness of their advice. But having money does not automatically make someone a great mentor. Mentoring requires a particular skill-set and making money is not top on the list. A mentor should be selected based on their ability to listen, interpret their mentee's needs and communicate solutions.

At the top of the list to be a great mentor is the ability to listen. Some may think this contradictory as mentors are known for giving advice. But mentorship is about giving advice based on a need. Author, Bryant H. McGill, states that one of the sincerest things you can do to demonstrate respect is the take time to listen, actually listen to what someone else has to say.

Great mentors elevate listening to an art form. They do not just hear the words that are spoken but they hear the heart of their mentee. They decipher conversational motives and meanings. They anticipate where the conversation is headed and not jump to the end of the conversation without listening to what their mentee is saying. A mentor can interpret what their mentee is trying to say. This is why great mentor/mentee relationships take time. They don't meet one day and have all the solutions the next day.

I am occasionally asked, "What is the difference between a mentor and a coach?' My answer in one word, relationship. A coach focuses on guiding their team members to a specific goal, focuses on the goal, helps a team member focus and sharpen their skills towards reaching a goal, target or destination. A mentor focuses on the person. Mentors develop their mentee's skills, focus, and effort towards creating a better person, who then in return, can reach their specific goal, target or destination.

Because a mentor works on developing the person, the ability to communicate solutions is vital. It's in the ability to communicate where worlds either collide or unite. A mentor can have the key to unlock the world's greatest secret in their mind but if they cannot communicate it, those keys will unlock nothing but frustration for an eternity. A mentor doesn't need to be a great orator. They simply need to be able to sincerely listen and then speak truth to the best of their ability. A great mentor asks deep, probing and introspective questions that allow a mentee to gain clarity and come to an understanding on their own. The ability to do this often stems from years of working with others. The best mentors are successful but that doesn't mean they have to be rich. The best mentors are those that care.

"Listen up guys" I cleared my throat taking a deep breath. "I know it's natural to think that people with money automatically make great mentors. But the truth is far from it. Let's consider a classic mentor-mentee relationship where the mentee has less money than the mentor and a mentor who changed the world.

"Who has heard of Alexander the Great?" A few hands shot up but most of the room remained silent.

"Alexander the Great was the King of Macedon and respectably one of the most successful military leaders in history. At the height of his power, the Macedonian Empire stretched from Egypt to India, covering over 2 million square miles." As I took a dramatic pause, I scanned the room to see if they were listening. I continued hoping my next sentence would catch them.

"Alexander became King of Macedon at age 20 and conquered the world before he was 30 years old." I see a glimmer in a few of their eyes. "Imperative to his success was his ability to reason, his geographical prowess, and his intricate knowledge of military history, all of which he learned from one of his mentors, the Greek philosopher, Aristotle."

Aristotle was hailed as a genius of his time in several subjects, including philosophy, astronomy, geometry, biology, and poetry. Philip of Macedon, Alexander's father, hired Aristotle and he mentored Alexander until age 16. He communicated his understanding in various fields but his most profound impact on young Alexander may have come from extensive back-and-forth conversation in the context of Greek philosophy and poetry. By engaging the future emperor and demanding the use of his intellect at an early age, Aristotle endowed Alexander with a unique sense of logic and intuition that far surpassed his peers.

Aristotle's knowledge empowered Alexander, not his money. The truth of it is that Aristotle's material wealth would never compare to Alexander's but the wealth of his knowledge helped changed the world.

A great mentor doesn't need to have vast amounts of material wealth but simply be wise. Wisdom can be defined as the application of knowledge. When one has knowledge about a subject and can effectively apply that knowledge to specific situations, and that outcome benefits a person(s), they can be defined as a wise person. This is what makes a great mentor. It is not recorded that Aristotle fought alongside Alexander but Aristotle's knowledge allowed Alexander to win multiple battles. It was Aristotle's knowledge that benefited Alexander.

This is how it should work with all mentors. It is their knowledge and how that knowledge can help you that is important. Expertise and knowledge should be at the top of the list when looking for a mentor.

Bonus Tip: When choosing a mentor, consider their experiences. The number in a mentor's bank account is less important than the quality of the mentor. A mentor shapes your perspective which is more valuable than money. A mentor will give you years of experience that you don't have to live through, and provides insight beyond your current knowledge. A singular piece of advice can propel your thinking that would normally take years of trial and error to learn.

Mentor Tip: Choosing a mentor takes time. To help facilitate the process, here is a short list of questions to ask yourself to assess a potential mentor, and use to help guide you in your search.

Mentoring Questions Checklist:

1. Is this a person I look up to? If so, why?
One of the first questions you should ask yourself, is this someone I admire because of their achievements and experience? Your ideal mentor should be someone who shares a similar professional outlook and has

accomplished the goals you hope to achieve.

2. Am I able to work well with this person?
Finding someone who you look up to is the first step. Another question you should ask is, can I work well with this person? It's critical that you are comfortable and trust that you can communicate well with the person.

3. Can this person guide me toward my goals?
Mentorship has a purpose. It should never just be a conversation. A critical question you should ask is, can this person guide me to my professional goals? Mentorship is about guidance; a mentor "walking" their mentee towards a specific set of goals. Finding out if a potential mentor can do this is very important. This is done by asking "hard" questions beginning with, "Have they reached your desired career goals? If not, why not?" You may have to ask your potential mentor this question, do it. You don't want to spend months meeting with a mentor who cannot take you where you need to go.

> "We make a living by what we get, we make a life by what we give."
>
> — *Winston Churchill*

Mentoring Myth 2

Mentors Give You All the Answers You Need

Mentors are placed in your life to help you. They guide, they offer advice and they direct you in making sound decisions, however, they don't just give you the answers to your questions. Simply providing the answer doesn't allow room for you to grow and growth for the mentee is what every mentor wants. A good mentor doesn't just want to give advice like a medical doctor prescribes prescriptions, "take two of these daily and call me in a week". Mentors want to pour into their mentees in a way that builds the mentees up, not for a moment, but for a lifetime. Now, you don't always have to follow a mentor's advice, but based on their experience and expertise, you should always listen to the advice and evaluate it.

"Just Give Me the Answers, Bro!"

Justin eased himself into the chair next to my desk. His large book bag slowly sliding off his right shoulder. I pause and look at the Pokémon sticker attached to the side, Pikachu grins back at me from the faded, well-worn sticker. I grin, matching my expression to Justin's who always seemed to have a permanent smile on his face.

"So how are things going with your mentor?" I had matched Justin with a mentor, Frank, who has a degree in business from a New York state university. Justin has dreams of earning a Master of Business Administration from NYU and taking over the world through entrepreneurship endeavors. I thought it would be a great match.

"This guy sucks," Justin stated as casually as he could. I smiled, humored by his statement.

"Tell me about the experience." I asked.

"Where do I start?" Justin said pointedly. "He never tells me anything, we just talk."

I paused then asked, "What do you mean all you do is just talk?"

I was perplexed and the sarcastic little man who lives in my head which I am quick to tell people I inherited so blame genetics, was thinking this kid's a space cadet. What else do you do in a meeting with your mentor but talk? Did he want to do a weekly doughnut-eating contest? I told the little man in my head to shut up so I could listen to what Justin was saying.

Justin began to explain, "We talk and talk but he doesn't give me the answers I need. He keeps trying to get me to do these little assignments, I want to scream dude just tell me what to do."

Justin's frustration is a common one. Very often speaking with individuals in mentoring relationships they state they're not getting what they want. They feel as if their mentor just doesn't understand what they need. Unfortunately, mentees choose to end the relationship because of their unfulfilled expectation of mentorship. Good mentors don't just answer your questions, they walk you towards the answers.

"Hello, Frank? It's Dr. Mike, you have a minute?"

"Yeah Doc, yeah, for you? No problem, what's up?" Frank cheerfully chimed.

I began with, "So I spoke to Justin a little while ago…" Frank jumped in before I finished.

"My man Justin! You know, he's a quiet kid. He doesn't talk much. I've been trying to get him to relax but he seems kind of tense. I guess that's just him."

I smiled. My mind was turning. I began to see the problem.

Frank, a seasoned mentor, who had a strong track record developing successful mentees didn't realize what was happening. Frank understood that at the core of mentorship lies trust. He was attempting to build trust with Justin through conversation. Frank wanted to ensure that Justin trusted him so when he said something that Justin may not agree with, he would not walk away. Frank was attempting to walk Justin slowly to the answers he wanted, however, Justin didn't want to walk, he wanted to run. Frank understood a fundamental truth in having a good mentoring relationship; mentoring is a conversation with a cause. More important than giving Justin the answer, Frank knew that good conversation would build trust and allow Justin to not only understand an answer but how to eventually find his answers.

Good mentoring occurs when the mentor demonstrates the ability to guide the mentee rather than give them the answer. Giving the mentee the answer does not promote the growth that is essential in successful mentor/mentee relationships.

About two weeks later, I followed up with Justin to see if he was still attending his mentoring sessions and to see how things were going.

"So, tell me, how are things going with Frank?"

"Pretty good, Doc." Justin exclaimed, I could hear the sounds of music and other voices in the background. Justin took a moment to find a quieter spot nearby where we could hear each other better. "Mr. Frank has a lot to offer. We had a good sit down and talked about the mentoring process as he called it. The whole time I thought he was trying to play me but he was just trying to get me to see the answers for myself." He laughed, "Hey man, I was missing it the whole time. He's got some good information, thanks doc."

Most novice mentees believe that a mentor's job is to provide the answers to their questions and that's understandable. From the mentee's perspective, their mentor should have all the answers they need, if not then why be mentored. In most cases, the mentor can answer all the questions but I heard it said once that it is better to teach a man to fish instead of giving him a fish. Mentoring facilitates the mentee's learning process.

A mentor provides their experience and expertise and then allows the mentee to combine it with their knowledge to come up with answers. I am not insinuating a mentee should not expect answers, but they should be prepared to work with their mentor to find solutions that work for their particular problem. The best mentors don't want to clone themselves but wants a mentee that appreciates their wisdom and is willing to listen. When they are synced, the mentor simply fills in the gaps of the mentee's skillset. To do this the mentor gives information and sometimes assign projects that will enhance the mentee's skills. Each bit of advice builds on itself. If a mentor was to simply give answers it would stump the mentee's growth, and in the end, cause them not to see their full potential.

Bonus Tip: One of the most valuable ways to learn a lesson is to learn from someone else's experience. Most mentors have a lifetime of experiences they want to share via lessons, stories, and anecdotes. Taking time to listen to a mentor's life experience can provide a life-changing perspective.

Mentoring Tip: Asking the right questions, without seeming intrusive, can be difficult. To aid you in this process I have listed a few "starter" questions to ask so that you maximize your time with your mentor by getting to the core of their experiences.

MENTORING MYTHS

Questions to maximize a Mentorship Relationship:

1. What would you do if you were me?
Be direct and honest. Don't waste time trying to impress your mentor with how smart you are. Tell them about your specific challenges, and ask for their recommendations.

2. Is this where you thought you would end up?
This question may get you a few hearty laughs. Very few people have a career that moves from point A to point B. Most experienced professionals take a scenic route in their careers. How they got there is usually an interesting tale with mistakes and revelations. Learn from them.

3. What used to be your biggest weaknesses?
This question will set you apart from other mentees. It also is a great question to determine if this person will be a good mentor. A good answer reveals the number one trait of a great mentor; self-awareness. If you feel this question is too intense, try softening it by asking, "What did you learn about yourself in the last six months?"

4. What are you most proud of?
Give your mentor a chance to "brag". They've achieved a lot so let them tell you about their experiences.

5. Who else would you recommend I connect with?
This question might be better served for later meetings when there is more trust. It can exponentially expand

your network. Sometimes the best source for other mentors is your existing one.

6. *What professional organizations are you associated with and in what ways?*

No one becomes a rising star in any industry without attending the right conferences and trade associations. A good mentor can help you filter out the best ones.

> "As Iron sharpens iron, and so one person sharpens another."
>
> — *The Bible*

Mentoring Myth 3

Mentoring Only Works Face-to-Face

The internet has expanded our ability to connect with people across the world. People can be connected from coast to coast and from continent to continent in a moment. Mentoring relationships have benefited from the same technology. Through the use of Skype, texts, emails, and Google Hangouts, mentors and mentees can connect all over the world, and yes, it's still mentoring.

The historic viewpoint of mentoring is one wherein a mentor and mentee meet face-to-face to discuss an issue or concern. A classic depiction is an older white man, perhaps gray-haired with spectacles, sitting with a young white man both dressed in business suits. Perhaps the older man has his jacket off and his sleeves are rolled up as he waxes eloquently about how the young man should proceed. The young man gazing in awe at the wisdom he is gleaning. The truth is that in the 21st century, mentoring relationships are far from this picture.

Mentoring takes place between men, women, young and old. Mentors and mentees are from vastly different backgrounds, ethnicities, and religions. The most drastic change has been in how mentoring takes place. With the use of technology, mentoring has expanded to connect individuals across regions, countries and even hemispheres. The reason this works is mentoring was never about the locality, it is about the relationship.

Communication helps to build relationships. It is the ability to create trusting, nurturing relationships that matter, not the technology used. Technology, at best, enhances the relationship by making the ability to communicate easier. Technology does not define the quality of the mentoring relationship. Strong healthy mentoring relationships are rooted in communication that is built on trust, how you communicate is less important.

"Mr. Telephone Man, something's wrong ..."

Rob walks through the large open area where a few students are gathered. He is smiling as usual and waves at the faces he recognizes. Rob is the type of man who could work a room. Stick him in a room full of people he doesn't know and within 30 minutes, half the room would be his new buddies. He prides himself on being the master of the face-to-face. It's his comfort zone. If the face-to-face was a kingdom, he was the supreme ruler. I heard him coming, we always hear him when he enters a room. I step out of my office and greeted him.

"Hey sir, how are you doing today?" I chimed. Smiling, he whispers, "I need to speak to you."

The smile on my face begins to dissipate bracing myself for what he would say. He was one of my most consistent and likable mentors. His dedication was stellar and I did not want to jeopardize losing him. We settled ourselves at my desk and waited. After what seems like an eon of shifting and settling, he begins.

"I can't meet with my mentee." He says. I can hear the frustration in his voice.

"Wow, Rob, I am so sorry to hear this, how come?" I said calmly but my head was spinning thinking of who I could match Rob with. I continued, "It is a personality thing? Are you guys bumping heads when you meet?" I was fishing for answers, as Rob never had a problem with any other mentee in the six years he's served as one of my mentors.

"Bump heads?" Rob said with a giggle, Rob realized I had misinterpreted what he meant when he said he couldn't meet with his mentee. "I haven't even seen the guy and we only spoke in our initial phone call to set up our weekly appointments."

Rob continued, "Every time I try to set up a meeting either he or I have to cancel. You know how busy my office gets, it's just so hard to have that face-to-face."

I tilted my head to the side and glance at Rob. He laughed knowing I was not going to accept that excuse, and without saying a word, I pulled out my phone and placed it between us. He glanced down then glance up, he glanced down and up at me again.

I spoke in a soft but firm voice.

"Rob, this young man needs you. Please find a way to speak with him. I know you love face-to-face communication but remember we are here to help by any means necessary which sometimes includes doing it differently than we had before."

Rob glared at me, not liking my passive-aggressive tactic of taking out my phone and placing it between us. Rob thrived on the interpersonal connections he made face-to-face. He loved that he could slap a back, shake a hand, and make eye-to-eye contact with another person. It was in these types of spaces Rob become himself. It was hard for him to shift. But looking at him in the moment, I felt that he heard my heart and knew I was right.

Mentors are willing to step outside their comfort zone in order the make the connection with their mentees. There are multiple ways that mentors and mentees can connect when meeting face-to-face. Technology has allowed us to carry mini-computers in our pockets. A mentor can do phone calls, video chats, and even text messaging. There is also a plethora of apps that promote messaging that can be used to stay connected.

Bonus Tip: Some form of mentoring can take place even if you and your mentor don't know each other personally. A mentor is someone whose advice you heed. If there's someone who you listen to and take their advice, they can be deemed a mentor. That being said, there are numerous ways to be mentored without a face-to-face meeting: books, podcasts, YouTube, Instagram, and other social media and internet-based mediums.

Mentoring Tip: Technology is always advancing itself and there seems to be a never-ending release of new apps that allow for ease of communication. Always lookout for new technology that allows you and your mentor/mentee to connect. It eases the process and maximizes both a mentor's or mentee's time.

"If I have seen further it is by standing on the shoulders of giants."

— *Isaac Newton*

Mentoring Myth 4

You Should Only Have One Mentor

No one person knows it all. It's a fact. Logically, we know this. We understand it in so many areas of our lives. We don't make an appointment with our medical doctor so we can ask about changing the brakes on our car. We don't expect our mail carrier to provide a professional answer about our taxes. No man has infinite knowledge so why would we expect our mentor to know it all? Since we know one mentor does not have all the answers then why wouldn't we look for multiple mentors to gain as much perspective and information to enrich our lives? When we limit ourselves to only one mentor at a time, we inadvertently limit ourselves by the expectation of our mentor to have all the answers. Multiple mentors allow access to multiple perspectives especially when each of our mentors has individualized specialties.

"No, no and no"

Julio was adamant, "I'm not doing that". His hands waved across his body in large slashing motions. "No, no and no." he continued, turning his head side to side to emphasize his displeasure. "That doesn't make sense to me so I am not doing it."

I sighed heavily. Julio was getting on my freaking nerves. I was hungry, really hungry and when I get hungry, I lose myself. For Julio's sake, I had to hold it together.

"Julio, what doesn't make sense about what I just said? Talk to me." I started letting out another loud and long sigh. I had been standing in my office with Julio for 20 minutes in what was supposed to be a 2-minute conversation. My right hand started to shake as I was so hungry and tired. Yes, I was hungry, tired, and getting a headache. I was trapped in a trifecta of hurt; tired, hungry, and a headache, all because Julio wasn't accepting what I had just proposed.

Julio breathed heavily to show his displeasure with what I said. "I already have a mentor and I am not getting another one. If my one mentor can't do what I need then I will leave him and get a new one. But I am not doing this two-mentor thing. It doesn't make any sense to me. One mentor is enough. A mentor is supposed to have all the answers to your questions that is what makes them qualified to be a mentor. If you can't answer all my questions then you are not supposed to be a mentor."

I composed myself to make sure I didn't sigh before speaking. "Julio, who told you that you could only have one mentor?" I needed to get to the root of this false belief Julio held on to so firmly.

"Aahhh, excuse me Dr. Rod but that just makes sense. Nobody has to tell you anything when it makes sense, you just know."

I could hear the sarcasm in his voice. I could feel

myself getting hungrier as the seconds ticked away. Standing there, feeling my stomach churning, I was in no mood for Julio's sarcastic tone. He is a smart student, involved in campus activities, held down a part-time job, and he has a very good GPA of 3.6, but he was overthinking what it meant to be mentored. I realized at that moment that Julio didn't want a mentor, he felt he was too smart for that. He wanted a savior, a superhuman who held enough knowledge to answer every question that he could ask, and if you couldn't answer all his questions then you didn't deserve to be his mentor.

"Julio, you're a math major right?" I asked flatly.

"Yes," he responded slightly confused by the question.

"Okay, great I have a question." I started firing up as much strength as I could not to seem irritated. "Tell me, what role 18th-century literature, primarily novels written by women, played in challenging the ideology that preconceived ideas of gender-based roles in the home enhanced domesticity?"

Julio stared at me, blank-faced and quiet. I thought we both had enough. It was time for me to end this and get some lunch.

"The point I am making is as good as you are in math, I don't expect you to answer a question I have about 18th century literature, which is not your area of expertise. It is similar to having a mentor. Every mentor has an area of expertise. I am trying to connect you to a second mentor that has the information you can use to enhance yourself. You can have two mentors as long as you understand what each mentor's area of expertise is, and you tap into their respective areas."

I looked intently at Julio, was he getting it? I wasn't sure. Julio just stared at me. He was thinking about what I said. He was replaying it over and over in his mind. Breaking it down from different angles and measuring it through the lenses of his truth. I started to think about cheeseburgers, onion rings, and pizza. Yes, pizza with extra cheese and a side of cheese fries with …

I heard Julio's voice, small, distant, but clear. He pulled me back from my food fantasy. "I'm not sure I'm buying this Doc." he said slowly and deliberately. I took a deep breath and sighed, this was going to take some time. So much for my stomach, I needed to take some time and walk Julio through this process.

The belief that someone can have only one mentor at a time is a common myth. Much like Julio's belief, it is rooted in the idea that having more than one mentor diminishes the effectiveness of their "first" or "primary" mentor. This is understandable as mentees can often develop a deep emotional connection with their mentor. Gaining a new mentor feels like an emotional affair. But this can't be further from the truth. Having multiple mentors can serve a multiplicity of purposes.

Multiple mentors allow you to receive guidance on different areas of your life. One mentor to map out your career strategy, another to help you develop your educational goals, and another to discuss your personal life. One person can't do all that and even if one person could, having more than one mentor provides multiple areas of expertise.

Having mentors that are diverse from you is fantastic. They provide a rich and unique perspective that is different from yours, adding to your worldview. But sometimes we need a mentor that truly understands our personal history. Having more than one mentor increases the likelihood that at least one mentor has faced a similar situation as the protégé is facing. It may not be exact but close enough to provide truly insightful advice. This can be incredibly helpful when trying to get an understanding on a situation that can be personal.

Bonus Tip: The key to having multiple mentors is to understand the purpose of each mentor. Having clear and concise mid-term and long-term goals for each mentor is crucial as it provides a template for each of your mentors to follow as they guide you.

Mentoring Tip: Create a list of what areas wherein you think you could use mentorship. These areas could be broken down into sections such as career, educational, skill-based, or self-care mentoring. Now take a moment to think about who might fit these areas. If you don't know enough people to fit all these areas, ask your friends, family members or associates if they know someone who might make a good mentor. Don't stop at making the list. Go and ask, "Would you mind being my mentor?" Don't be surprised if they all say yes.

> "The mind is not a vessel to be filled, but a fire to be kindled."
>
> — *Plutarch*

Mentor Myths

men·tor
/ˈmenˌtôr,ˈmenˌtər/
noun
1. an experienced and trusted adviser.

verb
2. advise or train (someone, especially a younger colleague).

Mentoring Myth 5

Mentoring Is a One-Sided Experience

Mentoring is not a one-sided experience and it is easy to see how one could think it is. Traditionally when people think of mentoring, they imagine a senior mentor passing on their knowledge, expertise, and experience to a more junior mentee. When you think of this type of relationship, mentoring seems to be an inequitable hierarchal relationship. It appears to be top-down and only the mentee is gaining from the relationship. However, as the world has changed and evolved, so has mentoring.

Today, mentoring is more of a two-way street than ever before. It's a two-way street in the sense of both mentor and mentee must come to the table to share and connect. Also, it's a two-way street in the sense that both the mentor and mentee have valuable information to share.

A rapidly changing consumer and business landscape, as well as the incessant march of technology means that we all need to lean on each other for specific knowledge, expertise, networks, and increasingly important, soft skills. Mentees, who are often younger, have their finger on the pulse of how the up and coming generation is thinking, feeling, and their worldviews.

For a mentor to have access to this type of

information is invaluable. It keeps your mind young and your skills fresh. Successful people who don't start to mentor others will over time lose touch with their excellence. Mentoring someone connects you back to the original you who became so excellent."

"Nah, I'm good"

"I would love to, but I don't have the time to mentor anyone," Joe explained. Standing in the middle of the hallway, students and staff shuffled past us oblivious to my dilemma, my angst, my torment… Okay, Mike, it is not that serious. I listened intently. Joe was a prospective mentor I was recruiting for my program. I've been working on getting Joe into the program for a few months. He's been very resistant and now I've finally cornered him for a conversation even if it was in the middle of a bustling hallway.

"So, Joe, tell me why are you so resistant?" I had to pin down his reasoning. I knew if I could get him to mentor a student or two, he would be exceptional. He was charismatic, outgoing and my students who took his classes raved about how passionate he is when he taught. I had to find a way to convince him.

"I told you my schedule is crazy." I heard his words but I listened to his heart. I pulled Joe to the side of the hallway and found a couple of empty chairs where we could sit.

"I know you are busy and I want to respect your time but what's the real reason you are not interested in mentoring." I paced myself and measured my words. I wanted to do my best to reach Joe. If I couldn't convince him then I'd move on, but I had to give it my best shot. Deep inside I knew Joe would be right for my program and if I could get to the bottom of his denial, maybe I could convince him.

Joe and I settled ourselves into our seats and positioned ourselves so we could hear each other even among the hustle and bustle of students making their way through the corridor.

Then Joe spoke, "Look, let me be honest." I grew slightly excited, here it comes I thought, the real reason he won't mentor one of my guys. "The pay-off is just not there. I've done this type of thing before and it's one-sided, I mean I want to help but I don't see the point."

Joe sounded exasperated. I heard his frustration and doubt. He meant what he was saying and honestly, I understood. Joe's one-sided experience can be a common one but that is usually based on the mentor's expectations. I needed to work closely with Joe to make sure he understood the full benefits of being a mentor. It may take time but I knew I could convince him.

"Mentoring Pays"

Many mentees believe that their mentor doesn't have much to offer but this couldn't be further from the truth. It is easy to identify the benefits that a mentee gains from being mentored. Mentees gain a world of knowledge, perspective, and insight far beyond their years. By default, mentoring relationships are inherently mentee focused. The mentorships are designed to help the mentee, not the mentor, however, they are not the only ones who glean from the experience.

Mentors gain a wealth of understanding, knowledge, and self-fulfillment from sharing their knowledge. Someone once stated "If you want to learn something read about it. If you want to master it, teach it." In many ways, mentors gain a deeper understanding of their expertise in a particular subject matter because they are called to explain it. I know as a mentor myself; one can find themselves pulling on information that has been dormant, resting in the recess of the mind waiting to be reactivated. We pull information, ideas, and strategies that have not been used for years. We brush them off, reevaluate their usefulness and repurpose them for today's market with the hopes our mentees will find them beneficial. This act forces us to assess our tactics and ideas, creating a better understanding of the concepts we are putting forth.

Another benefit that mentors gain is an increased profile for themselves and the profile of their organization for serving as a mentor. Anyone who has mentored knows it takes time and we all know time is a premium commodity for most of us. To take time away from a normally busy schedule to pour into someone else can be seen as noteworthy. Not only from a personal point-of-view but from an institutional perspective. To boil it down to brass tacks, it looks good to others to serve as a mentor and we all, at some point in our career, want to look good.

Additional reasons to being a mentor: enhancement of people skills in areas such as leadership, interpersonal and communication. Finding unique ways to communicate your message, often to a person a generation younger than yourself is a challenge, but one, when met with the resolved to find a way to get it done, is highly rewarding. Also, that younger person you are mentoring just may be a professional in your field. Mentoring creates great networks by expanding your knowledge down to a younger generation.

The most important reason to mentor, in my opinion, is the intrinsic value derived from the personal satisfaction gained from making a difference to the career development of another person. It just feels good to help another person especially when they are in no position to help you. As a mentor, you have given of yourself with no realistic expectation of a return from the person you are helping. You have stepped out of yourself and given of your time and knowledge just because you want to. At the end of the day, what reward could be greater than an act of kindness with no expectation of reward?

Bonus Tip: Let me be clear, mentoring is hard work. It takes time, mental energy and a focus that can be draining. But the exchange of information between mentor and mentee is invaluable for both. For a mentor, being exposed to new ideas and new perspectives is a goldmine. Understanding how the next generation thinks, helps the mentor better understand the emerging world of work.

Mentoring Tip: To help facilitate the mentoring process and allow the mentor to view you as a resource there is one question that should be asked. It could be asked after a session or two so that both of you are comfortable with each other but it should be asked early in the mentorship relationship.

#1 Mentoring Question for a Mentee to ask a Mentor

1. *What can I do for you?*

This question may catch your mentor by surprise. In mentorship relationships rarely will the mentee ask this question, but you should. It will set you apart and demonstrate that you are there not just to take from the mentor but also add value where you can.

> "I am not a teacher,
> but an awakener."
>
> — *Robert Frost*

Mentoring Myth 6

Mentoring Doesn't Get "Real" Results

I've heard it before. I've heard it from students, staff, and faculty members as well as from supervisors, mid-level managers, and senior staff executives. They all have said the same thing, "Mentoring is a nice thing to do but it doesn't get real results." They are wrong. I say confidently and assuredly, "Mentoring gets results." Mentoring done right, can directly shape organizational outcomes. Mentoring can and does affect the bottom-line. But, how you may ask. Mentoring encourages retention, improves productivity, and enhances professional development to name a few.

"Let's not talk about the Kelvin incident"

Reggie tugs on his jacket as he takes a seat. It's a nervous tick he developed in high-stress situations. He wanted this promotion…no, he needed it this promotion. With two children in college next year, the raise that would come with the new position would help tremendously. "Man, the boys can eat," he thought to smile at the hiring committee.

John Greene, chair of the committee smiled back at Reggie. Samantha Smith and Wayne Trevor also smiled back at him. "Well Mr. Bolton, we've gone through the first round of interviews and we are glad to have you back for…," John pauses and in his best boxing ring announcer voice belts out the phrase,

"Welcome to round two." He laughed heartily and two other committee members joined in. Reggie chuckled and thought to himself, "This is going to be fun."

John still smiling continued, "Reggie, we would love to hear what new initiatives you would bring to Health Corps Services if you were selected as the next Executive Director of Strategic Initiatives. Reggie took a quiet breath and began.

"I'm not going to sugar-coat my response," he said flatly.

John perked up, "Please don't, I'd love to hear it straight." glancing at Paul and Lisa. He was intrigued.

Reggie smiled as he spoke the next few sentences, "I have been with this company for over ten years and I have worked in nearly every capacity and we have a problem. Health Corps is having trouble recruiting qualified employees, especially for our entry-level positions. I have one word that will solve that problem." He paused for emphasis, "Mentoring."

Samantha jumped in, "didn't we have a mentoring program about 5 or 6 years ago?" John and Wayne shook their heads in agreement.

"Yes, we did," Reggie continued, "But that was an informal program designed to improve company morale after the Kelvin incident." John, Wayne, and Samantha shuffled nervously in their seats. There was a silent agreement among senior staff to never bring up the Kelvin incident.

Reggie noted the tension in the air and continued, "I am not going to talk about the Kelvin incident, but I will address why that program didn't work. Fundamentally, that program was a reactionary response to an incident that didn't address the root problem. I am proposing a mentoring program that targets the top three feeder colleges for Health Corps. The program would match students interested in the allied health field with professionals at Health Corps. The students would get real-world experience and insider knowledge at one of the biggest and the best health care organizations in the region. They would also get the opportunity to apply first for any new job opportunities, and let's be honest, based on the latest results from our applicant pool, we could use more qualified applicants. The employees would get a thank you letter for their file, a certificate of completion, and perhaps a free lunch at the end of the year. Best of all, they would only need to commit one or two hours a week."

John sat back in his chair and placed his hand on his chin, "Tell me more about this program." Reggie leans forward and continues. He was ready to hit them with the good stuff.

"Do You Really Get Results?"

Reggie pulls into his parking spot. He looks up he reads the placard in front of his parking space, "Parking Space Reserved for the Executive Director of Strategic Initiatives." He smiles and thinks, "Wow, it's been thirteen months." Sliding out his car and heading towards his office he glances to his right and sees John Greene. John is doing a slow jog toward Reggie. He slows down so John can catch up.

John smiles and gives a panting "Good morning, Reggie." John pauses to catch his breath then continues, "You know I had some misgivings about this mentoring program you mentioned in your interview but I have to say I am pleasantly surprised, you get results!"

Reggie, motioned to John, "Let's walk and talk," Reggie and John headed toward their offices.

"The secret to mentoring is kind of simple. Mentoring improves relationships. Better relationships lead to better-engaged clients. A "client" that Health Corps wasn't serving was a potential future employee. Mentoring allows our future employees to be "a part" of our organization before their first paycheck. They feel like part of the company because we've been fortunate to create buy-in with them over the past year. I'm not sure you received my last report passed around in the last executive meeting, but just look at the first mentoring cohort we developed last year. Out of seventy-eight mentees, we've received fifty-two viable applications. You see, the better we engage, prepare and expose potential employees to our culture, the better it is for us and them because they feel like Health Corps is home."

John tapped Reggie on the shoulder and heads to his office, and says "Well, the results speak for themselves. Mentoring those college students did yield a strong pool of applicants. No one can deny that. I just wonder what you'll do for an encore."

Reggie smiles and responds, "Studies have shown that mentees are more fulfilled and find their work more rewarding. These studies have taken place in educational settings, healthcare systems, and business organizations. We are not stopping once they get in the door, John. Just wait to see what type of employees we start producing once we start mentoring them."

Bonus tip: Building a mentoring program is daunting but the results can be significant. For an organizational-based mentoring program to work, buy-in is needed at all levels. Before attempting to build one, make sure you have support from key stakeholders throughout the organization.

Mentoring tip: Before designing a mentoring program for your organization, decide what results you want to achieve. Be specific. Is it designed to increase student retention at your school? Do you want to recruit new employees to your company? Or perhaps you want to retain and train better-qualified employees for the senior-level positions in your organization. It is all possible. Just make sure your mentoring program's goals are clear and concise.

Bonus Chapter
3 Bonus Mentoring Tips

There are tons of myths about mentoring. Take a survey on the street and every person you speak with; you'll hear a different myth. Combine with the fact I love to write and this book could be volumes just talking about the many myths that plaque the ideology of mentoring. But I want to leave you with three myths that I think are important to touch on.

I often hear these three myths when speaking to deans, directors, supervisors or someone from an organization's senor staff. These myths appear when discussing the development of organizational mentoring programs, one of my specialties. There is no doubt in my mind that any organization can and will benefit from a formalized mentoring program. Mentoring not only works with individuals but it can also change an organizations culture, productivity and outcome.

Bonus Mentoring Myth #1:
Mentoring Relationships Can't Be Measured

Good mentoring is goal-oriented. The mentor and mentee work together to achieve a predetermined goal. In formalized mentoring programs, organizational leaders set the objectives by answering the question, "Where do we want our people to be and when do we want them to get there?" Programmatic measurement is based on what the mission or objective the organization wants to achieve. They can be short or long-term in nature and most importantly, they can be measured.

Bonus Mentoring Myth #2:
Results Happen Overnight

There is an adage that says "Rome was not built in a day." Well, neither are great mentoring programs. When building a mentoring program, you need time to implement, manage, and assess the program's effectiveness. An effective program is malleable and not only fits an organization's needs but compliments the organizational culture— this takes time. Just as it takes time to build rapport among mentors and mentees, it will take time to build your mentoring program. Given enough time to mature, you will have a great organizational asset.

Bonus Mentoring Myth #3:
Mentoring Stops Once A Goal Is Reached

To have an effective mentoring program, you must be willing to work the program until your goals are met but you don't stop the program just because a goal has been achieved. You simply set new goals! Your organization is a dynamic, ever-evolving entity and your mentoring program should reflect that truth. As organizational goals adjust, so should your mentoring program goals.

Final Thoughts
Mentoring Works

I opened this book talking about the years my fears and misunderstandings about mentoring stopped me from being mentored. I missed educational and career opportunities because I allowed my fear to feed me instead of my faith. As I conclude this book, I hope any fear you had about being mentored have been alleviated.

Mentoring is a tool, use it. Drop all fears you have about approaching someone to mentor you. Let go of the distrust you have about that senior-level executive on the job that seems interested in helping you, and let them help you. Embrace it, formalize it and work it. Gain all the knowledge and skills you can from your mentors and soar into your wildest dreams.

I believe mentors are sent to you to take you to your next level. I encourage you to take a look at the areas in your life where you want to improve and find someone who can mentor you into your new level of success. Trust me, once you have opened yourself up to being mentored you will attract the mentors you need.

Don't allow the small murmurs of distrust, fear, and intimidation speak to you. They are the voices of the unaccomplished. When you give in to these voices, you settle for being less than you are meant to be. Fear has no place in you or your future.

I know it's not easy to shift gears from paralyzing fear to full throttle faith but even in this type of transition, a mentor can help you. If you suffer from a deep fear of seeking out a career or college mentor, then I suggest you start with someone close to you to recommend a mentor.

All of us have a few people who we can confide in. They may not be able to serve as a mentor to you, depending on your goals, but they can serve as a connector to a possible mentor. Reach out to them and have a discussion. Tell them what you want to be and where you desire to reach, and ask them if they know anyone you can speak with. You may find out that the phrase "six degrees of separation", which is the idea that all people are six, or less, social connections away from each other, is true. Start today, don't delay. Set yourself on the path to becoming your greatest self through mentorship.

Acknowledgements

I wrote my first story in seventh grade. I have been writing, in one form or another, ever since. Within all that time, my greatest muse has been the love of my life, my wife, Marie. Thank you for your encouragement, support, advice, and love. It has fueled me to do more than I ever thought I could accomplish. From a bike messenger to a Doctorate of Education you have been my constant cheerleader. I love you more than words can say.

To my family and friends at my home church, Dabar Bethlehem Cathedral, thank you. To Bishop H. Curtis Douglas, thank you for your constant support and encouragement. Your prayers and kind words have been heard and received.

To Pastors Keith and Andrea Heyward at my Virginia Church, Dabar Christian Center. We are a family. The years of prayers, laughter, and love have lifted and loosed me. I am grateful for your love and support. The time Marie and I have spent with you both, Mother Ruthie, Ashlee, and Amber, means the world to me.

To Pastor Tyrone and Pamela Zimmerman of Latter Rain Christian Fellowship, I say, thank you. What began as friendship transformed into family. Your friendship is invaluable and you trusting and sharing your daughters, Brianna and Shaina, has blessed me in more ways than I can say.

To the members of the "Final Four" Bernard, Lori and Karen. We were connected by fate, grew in faith and have lived our lives in love through our common experiences. I love you all. Let's keep standing.

To all the mentees who have become friends, Gerald, Ronish, Javon, Kaiqwon, Eddy, and my MRC family too many of you to name all. Thank you for allowing me to speak into your life. I've grown tremendously with the experience I have had with each of you.

To my mentors, Professor Kenneth Wheeler, Professor Orlando Warren, Professor Martin Simmons, Dr. Marcia Cantarella, Dr. David Gomez, Dr. Leah Georges, and the countless numbers of people who have poured into me over my life time I say from the bottom of my heart, thank you!

About the Author

Michael P. Rodriguez, Ed.D. aka "Dr. Rod" is a leading educational expert who works on the topics of student development; equity, diversity, leadership and male development.

He's been a featured guest on the national podcast The Chip Baker Success Chronicles, the syndicated radio talk show The Tom Pope Show as well as local radio in the NYC area. He's been highlighted by the City University of New York's Black Male Initiative program for his ongoing work; developing mentoring and leadership programs for African American and Latino males.

Michael comes from modest means and college became a way out. He took advantage of this opportunity and changed the trajectory of his life. He is dedicated to helping others use education as a tool towards their success. To that end, he has worked with students from underserved communities, helping them use education as a way to find success, particularly at the Community College level. Michael has been acknowledged for his work as an exceptional advisor and has been the recipient of awards for outstanding achievements several years in a row, and also earned multiple faculty achievement awards working within the City University of New York for the past 12 years.

MICHAEL 'DR. ROD" RODRIGUEZ

As Executive Director of Empowering Minds for Tomorrow, a 501(c)(3) nonprofit organization, Michael and his partners are dedicated to helping others overcome their barriers to success, specifically barriers to educational and career success. Michael is passionate about his work as a mentor and to that end is trained in Adult Mental Health First Aid, Certified by the Mental Health First Aid (MHFA) of USA.

He is proud to be Jesuit educated with an earned Doctorate of Education degree from Creighton University, ranked the #1 Best College in the Midwest by U.S. News. He holds a Master of Arts, from Long Island University and a Bachelor of Arts, from the College of New Rochelle.

As an author, professional speaker, mentor, and co-founder of Empowering Minds for Tomorrow, Michael has spoken to thousands of students both nationally and internationally.

Michael loves to read; write, workout, volunteer at his church and spend quality time with his wife, Marie.

Find more information about Michael on his website
www.dr-rod.com

or at other Social Media:

Instagram at: **dr_mike_rod**
Facebook: **Dr. Michael Rodriguez**
Twitter: **MichaelMichaelP**

A Few of My Mentees

Two of the coolest guys I've mentored, Gerald Maître, MSW, (center) and Eddy Roland, (right). Both worked with me to change hundreds of lives in the Men's Resource Center, a part of the City University of New York's (CUNY) Black Male Initiative (BMI) Program at Kingsborough Community College.

Harry Tan (center) and Cid Dominique (right) are doing some amazing things in their careers. Harry is making a major impact in the health field, and Cid is a rising star as the head of Delivery Service for a major IT business management consulting firm in New York.

Actor, Rapper, Activist and Director, Moise Morancy, is truly a gifted young man. He is a mover and shaker in the world of entertainment. Be on the lookout for what he's doing next.

Roman V. Charnolusky is a gifted problem solver. His intellect and keen socio-emotional intellect, makes him a fantastic mentee who constantly challenges me to push myself as a mentor. He is making waves as an operations consultant.

This is an awesome group of young men I mentor at my home church, Dabar Bethlehem Cathedral (DBC) in Queens Village, New York. The program called, *The Ananias Initiative*, consists of a multiplicity of workshops concentrating in four areas: Spiritual Enrichment, Academic Development, Career Preparation, and Leadership Instruction.

Here I am with a two of the many incredible groups of young people I've mentored at Kingsborough Community College Men's Resource Center, a part of the City University of New York's (CUNY) Black Male Initiative.

Thanks for reading!

Please submit a short review on Amazon and let me know your thoughts!

Thank you from the bottom of my heart and God bless you.

Michael "Dr. Rod" Rodriguez, Ed.D.

www.ingramcontent.com/pod-product-compliance
Lightning Source LLC
Chambersburg PA
CBHW060343080526
44584CB00013B/891